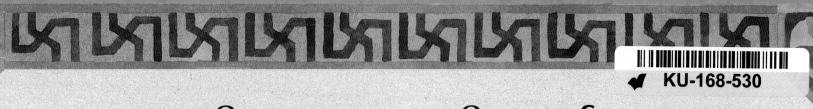

इसलामी कला की पूर्ण यात्रा

Journey through Islamic Art

Na'ima bint Robert & Diana Mayo

mantra

मैनें समरकन्द और बग़दाद शहर के किस्से सुने,
भारत में मुग़लों और स्पेन में मूरों के बारे में भी।

I heard tales about the cities of Samarkand and Baghdad,
About the Moghuls in India and the Moors in Spain.

मैनें इतिहास के रेशमी धागे अपने हाथों में समेटे और,
उससे, मेरे दिमाग ने एक उड़ता लबादा बुनाः
एक लबादा जो मुझे इस्लामीं संसार के कला
की एक आश्चर्यजनक यात्रा कराए।

I gathered silken threads of history in my hands and,
With them, my mind wove a flying cloak:
A cloak that took me on an amazing voyage
Through the art of the Islamic world.

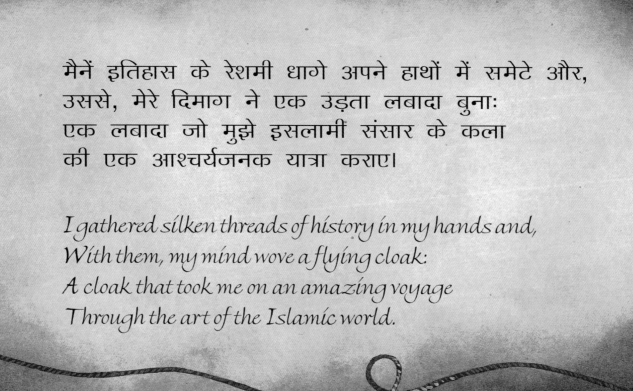

मेरा लबादा मुझे पुराने बग़दाद शहर में ले गया,
जो मसजिदों, सार्वजनिक स्नानघरों,
घुड़दौड़ के रास्ते तथा प्रदर्शनीयों का घर था।

My cloak took me to the old city of Baghdad,
Home to mosques, public baths,
racetracks, and pavilions.

मजबूत रेगिस्तानी किले का घर,
जो फर्श से लेकर छत तक चित्रकारी से सजा था।
दुनिया के सबसे बड़े मसजिद समारा का घर,
मुझे लगा जैसे प्रार्थना की पुकार मेरे पास
बादलों तक पहुँच गयी।

Home to fortified desert castles,
Adorned with wall-paintings from floor to ceiling.
The largest mosque in the world called Samarra its home,
I imagined that the call to prayer reached me in the clouds.

मेरा लबादा मुझे मुसलिम स्पेन ले गया,
जहाँ पूरब पश्चिम से मिलते।
मैं वैज्ञानिक, आविष्कारक तथा राज्य ज्योतिषी से गुजरा,
जिन्होने इन्सान के ज्ञान की सीमा को परखा।

My cloak took me to Muslim Spain,
Where the East met the West.
I passed scientists, inventors and court astronomers,
Testing the limits of human knowledge.

वहाँ, सजे आंगन में सैर की,
फौवारों और सुगन्धित बागों से गुजरी।

There, I wandered through ornamental courtyards,
Past fountains and scented gardens.

इस्लाम की कला की
विरासत और स्पेन ने
मिलकर अल हमबरा
महल और
कोरडोबा की महान
मसजिद को बनाया।
गुम्बद, रंगीन काँच
और मेहराबदार रास्तों
ने मेरी बेचैन आँखों
का स्वागत किया।

The artistic heritage
of Islam and Spain
Fused to create the
Al Hambra palace and
the great mosque
of Cordoba.
Domes, mosaics and
archways greeted my
eager eyes.

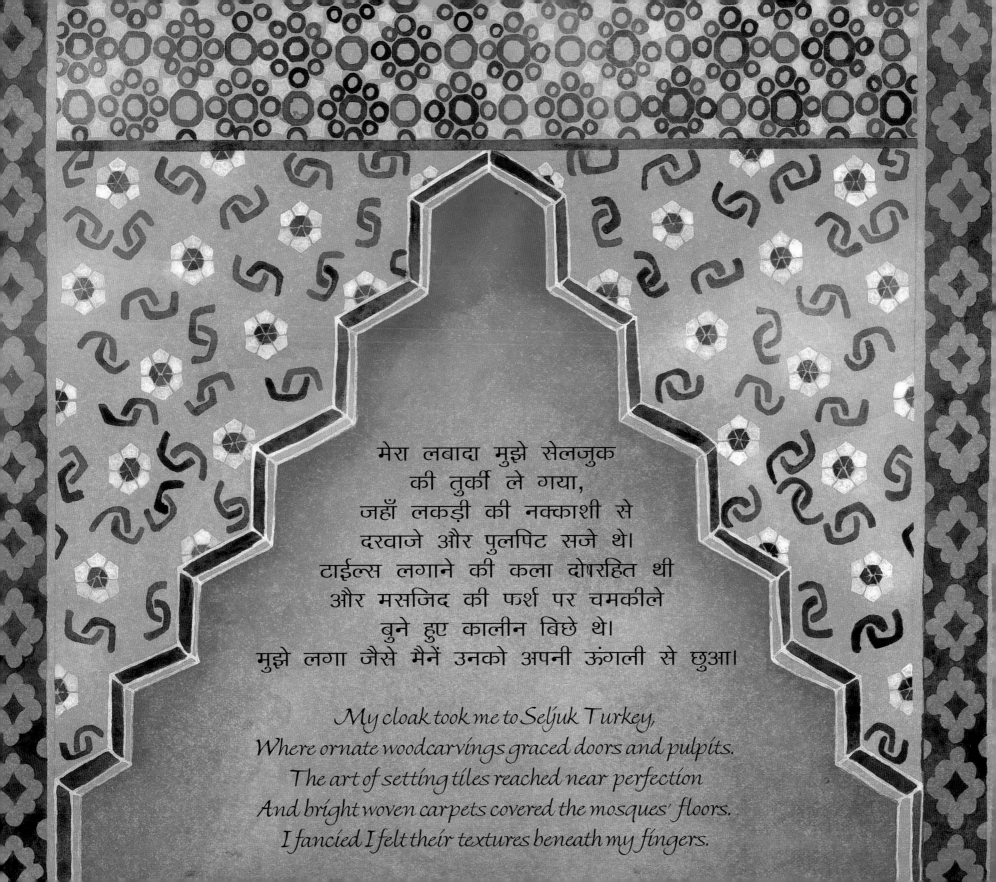

मेरा लबादा मुझे सेलजुक
की तुर्की ले गया,
जहाँ लकड़ी की नक्काशी से
दरवाजे और पुलपिट सजे थे।
टाईल्स लगाने की कला दोषरहित थी
और मसजिद की फर्श पर चमकीले
बुने हुए कालीन बिछे थे।
मुझे लगा जैसे मैनें उनको अपनी उंगली से छुआ।

My cloak took me to Seljuk Turkey,
Where ornate woodcarvings graced doors and pulpits.
The art of setting tiles reached near perfection
And bright woven carpets covered the mosques' floors.
I fancied I felt their textures beneath my fingers.

मेरा लबादा मुझे तैमूर
'लंगड़े' के समरकन्द ले गया,
जहाँ पूरी दुनिया के कारीगर
जमा किए गए।

*My cloak took me to the Samarkand
of Timur 'the Lame'
Where artisans from around the world
were gathered.*

भारत से राजगीर,
इरान से सुलेख लिखने वाले,

Stonemasons from India,
calligraphers from Persia,

तुर्की से सुनार तथा दमिश्क से
रेशम की बुनाई करने वाले।

*Silversmiths from Turkey and
silk-weavers from Damascus.*

अपने शहर को सुन्दर बनाने के लिए,
सभी को बन्दी बना कर लाया गया,
जब की उसका अपना महल एक तम्बू था
- अन्त तक एक खानाबदोश की तरह

All brought back as captives, to beautify his city,
While his palace was a tent - a nomad to the end.

मेरा लबादा मुझे आगरा की सड़कों पर ले गया,
जहाँ ताजमहल के बारे में बाजार में अफवाह उड़ रही थी।

My cloak took me to the streets of Agra,
Where rumours of the Taj Mahal filled buzzing bazaars.

एक मृत्यु शैया पर दी हुई कसम से एक इमारत पैदा हुई,
यह सफेद संगमरमर का पहनावा है जो
रोशनी में झिलमिलाता है।

A building born from a deathbed promise,
Its garment of white marble
Shimmered in the light.

المشرق

कुरान के खुदे हुए सुलेख,
फूलों की तरह अरबी लिखी तथा रेखागणित
का खाका आपस में मिले हुए
और जिसे कवि 'भोर का सुनहरा चेहरा' कहते हैं।
काश इसकी खूबसूरती जिवित का उपकार करे
और मरे हुए का पूज्य स्थल न बने।

صباح الفجر

Calligraphic inscriptions from the Qur'aan,
Floral arabesques and geometric designs
all harmonised
And the poets named her 'Dawn's bright face'.
I wished its beauty could grace the living
and not enshroud the dead.

यह यात्रा एक सपना थी,
एक बच्चे की कल्पना थी,
जब की सभी जगहें वास्तविक थीं।
मुझे आशा है आप का लबादा इस
कहानी से बुन जाएगा
और वहाँ आप भी जाएंगे।

This voyage was a dream - a child's fantasy,
Though all its destinations are true.
I hope that your cloak will be spun by this tale
And that you will go there too.

Here are some explanations to help you enjoy the story:

Samarra
In the 9th century, after the foundation of Baghdad, the Caliph (ruler) moved his capital to the splendid city of Samarra.
The Great Mosque was once the largest mosque in the Islamic world and rises to a height of 52 meters.

Islamic Spain was established in the 8th century by Muslims from North Africa who were known as Moors. For over three
hundred years, Muslims, Christians and Jews lived together in a Golden Age when learning, art and culture flourished.

Seljuk Turkey was one of the eras in Islamic history. The Seljuks were Muslim rulers who took control of Persia and
Turkey. Seljuk Turkey became the centre of excellence in weaving, ceramic painting and wood carving.

Born in the 14th century, **Timur 'the Lame'**, also known as Tamerlane, was a fierce and determined Mongol warrior
who loved art. Whenever his armies invaded foreign cities, he would take care to protect the artisans and take them back
to beautify his city, Samarkand.

The **Taj Mahal** was a monument built by the Mughal Emperor Shah Jahan in 1631 as a tribute to his loving wife Mumtaz
Mahal. Legend says that she made him promise to build her a mausoleum more beautiful than any the world had ever seen.

Arabesque is an art form originally from Asia Minor. It was later adapted by Muslim artisans into a highly formalised form
of intertwined flowers and plants.

The Qur'aan, the Muslim holy book, was revealed to the Prophet Muhammad (pbuh) by the Angel Gabriel. Its verses are
often inscribed in beautiful patterns by calligraphers.

First published in 2005 by Mantra Lingua
Global House, 303 Ballards Lane, London N12 8NP
www.mantralingua.com

A CIP record for this book is available from the British Library.

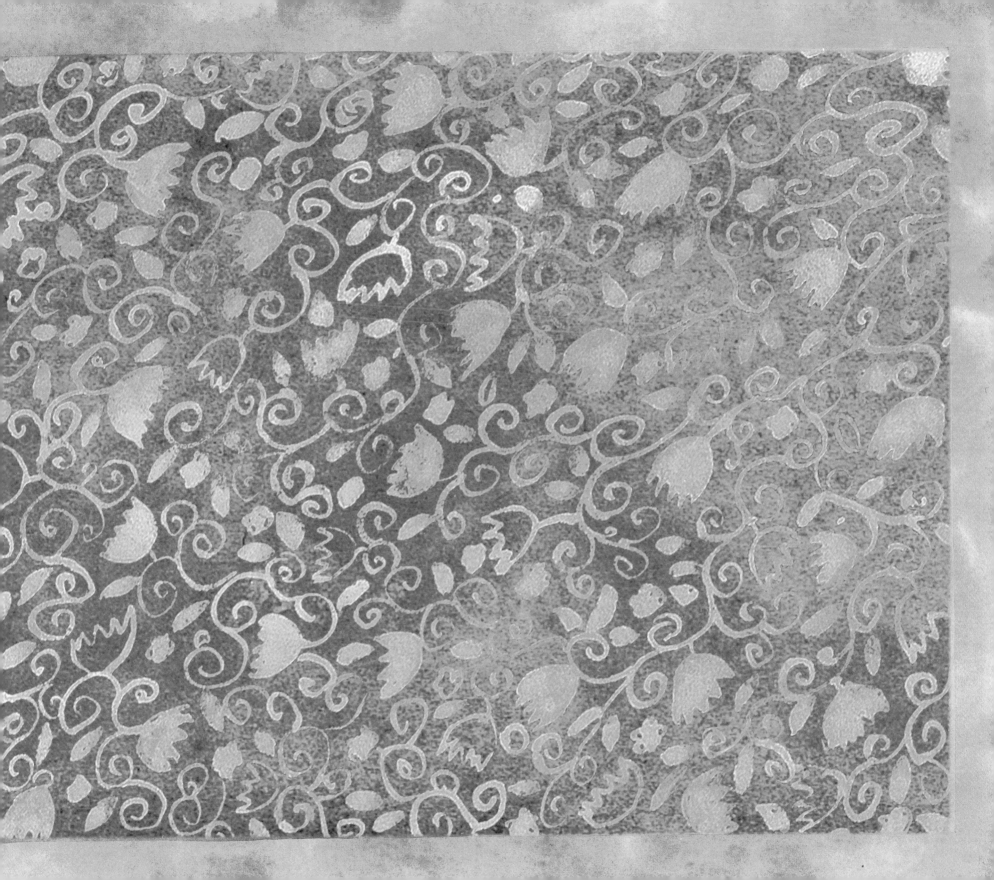

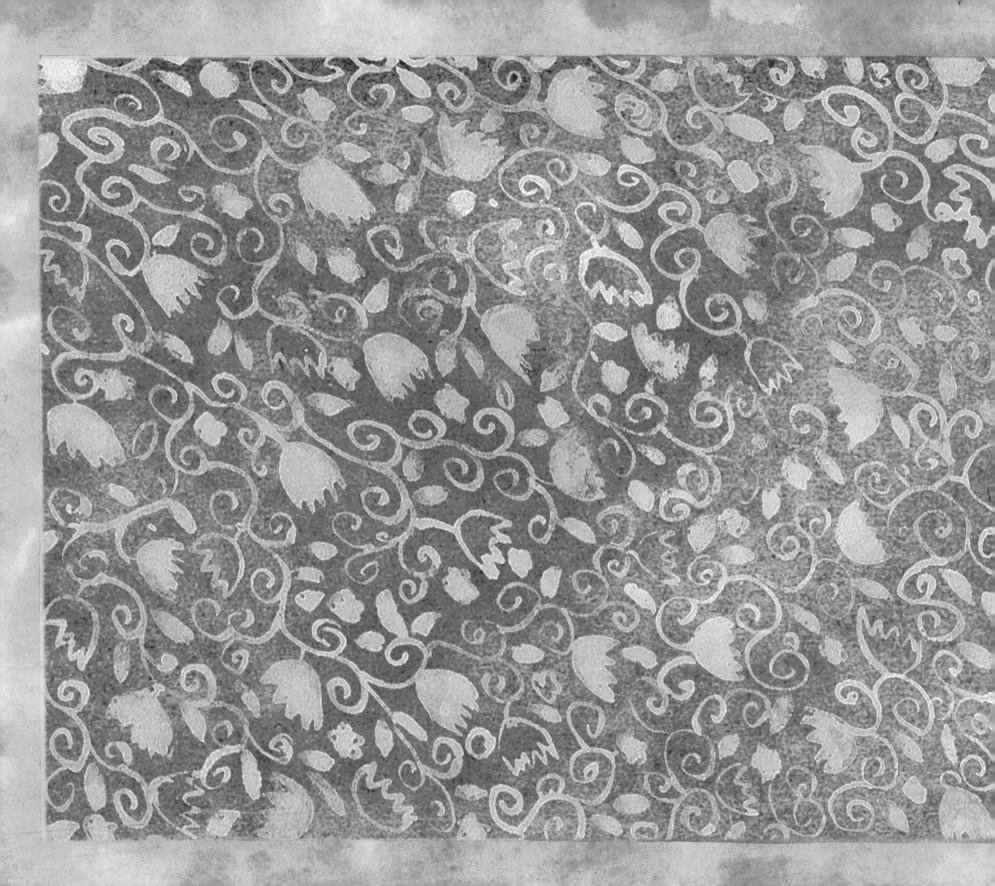